THE BEST MAN'S
DUTIES

Also available from Elliot Right Way Books

Wedding Speeches
Wedding Etiquette Properly Explained*
Sample Social Speeches
Right Joke For The Right Occasion
Apt & Amusing Quotations

*By the same author

THE
BEST MAN'S
DUTIES

Vernon Heaton

RIGHT WAY

Contents

1

Introduction

I wonder how many men accept, on the spot and without consideration, the invitation of a very close friend to be the best man at his wedding?

Too many, probably, will jump at the offer with delight, seeing ahead of them the tempting opportunity to pull the leg of a best friend and to become the leader in all the customary pranks that have long been associated with engagements and weddings. To encourage and assist friends in stuffing the bridegroom's suitcases with confetti so that when they are opened in the honeymoon hotel, the confetti will burst forth in a cloud; to tie a collection of tin cans and old shoes to the back of the 'going away' car, together with streamers, balloons, foam and a 'Just Married' sign, all designed to draw the attention of passers-by to the embarrassed occupants; and to string together a few facetious comments as a speech to be given at the reception, so as to raise as much laughter as possible at the expense of the newly-weds.

Not many men know enough about the duties of the

best man to give such an invitation sufficient thought
before agreeing to accept the task.

In fact the best man may be expected to act as a
master-of-ceremonies, as a chief marshal in charge of
the ushers, a toast-master, dispenser of oil on troubled
waters, paymaster, messenger, persuader, remembrancer,
chief liaison officer between the bridegroom and the
bridal contingent — and a repository for such valuables
as the wedding ring, cash, documents for the honeymoon
— and lost property.

To those of you who have, wittingly or unwittingly, agreed to shoulder the responsibilities of escorting a bridegroom to his wedding, I dedicate the following chapters; and to those who have not yet been dragooned into accepting the 'honour' — be warned!

2

Qualifications

The choice of the best man is the sole prerogative of the bridegroom. Not even the bride has the right to interfere — though it is not unknown for her wishes to influence a final choice!

Though there was no rule about the matter, it was customary in the past to make the choice from single men; however nowadays many best men are themselves already married.

A man's best friend is the almost universal selection for the honour — be he brother, more distant relative or life-long companion.

But it takes all sorts to make a world and the bridegroom's closest friend may not have all the skills necessary for such an important task.

Before the offer is made, therefore, the bridegroom should give careful consideration to the following points concerning his proposed choice:

(a) Is he eager and happy to accept the duty — or is he merely going to do it 'if he has to'?

(b) Has he the ability and the necessary enthusiasm to help carry out the detailed task of organising the event — and of dealing with the practical tasks that arise?

(c) Can he make a speech without being a bore?

(d) Is he quick-witted enough to deal with an emergency? Such as when the nervous bridegroom drops the wedding ring; the bride fails to turn up on time; the clergyman gets his dates

Is the best man quick-witted enough?

mixed up and they arrive to find the church door locked against them?!

Though unlikely, such slip-ups do occur from time to time.

(e) Can he be relied on to safeguard the ring and the other items that will come under his charge? And will he remember where he is keeping them?

Other points must also be taken into account, such as:

(a) Does he get on well-enough with the bride? Although the selection of best man is no real concern of hers, obviously the groom won't want to upset her by choosing someone whom she doesn't like.

(b) Is he certain to be available to take part in the ceremony on the date and will he have time to help in the pre-planning and practical arrangements that must be made in advance? If he is not able to help with the pre-wedding arrangements, the groom may need to appoint a 'chief usher' (see Chapter 3, page 15).

The chosen best man should give as much thought to the question of accepting the role as the bridegroom has given to his selection. He should know even better than the groom of any impediment that might prevent him from performing his duties successfully. Perhaps he has not the time at his disposal to give full attention to the event; maybe he feels that the responsibility is too onerous for him; and possibly he just imagines the role too uncomfortable for his liking.

If he has any doubt about either the propriety or wisdom of accepting the bridegroom's invitation, he should decline at once. The decision must not be left to the last minute; nor should he change his mind at the last minute which would leave the groom with little chance of finding a replacement.

3

The Ushers

As arrangements for the wedding must be made some time in advance of the event, it is necessary for the bridegroom to nominate his best man as soon after the engagement is announced as is possible and convenient.

It does sometimes happen, however, that the chosen best man lives far from the bridegroom and out of touch with day-to-day events. He may be a 'best friend' who is studying or working far away — perhaps even a member of one of the Services and possibly stationed overseas. He may, because of such circumstances, be able to travel to the venue of the wedding and to stay there for just a few days — perhaps for the day of the wedding only.

Yet, despite the difficulties and frustrations involved, the bridegroom may hold this particular friend or relative in such high esteem that he is unwilling to be escorted to his wedding by anyone else.

The answer to the problem is the appointment of another friend — possibly the 'next best friend' — as

The need is to have sufficient ushers...

chief usher. The choice of such an individual should be made by consultation between the bridegroom and the best man, bearing in mind that:

(a) He must be willing, capable and have the time to act as deputy to the best man during probably the whole of the preliminaries.

(b) He must be well known and a friend of the bridegroom as they will be involved together in

The bride's relatives.

making the arrangements and carrying out the practical details.

(c) He must be a close friend of the best man who will expect him to have ready, and be able to turn over to him with the shortest of briefings, all the information and items he will require for the wedding.

The duties of the chief usher are, of course, those of the best man, up to and until the best man is available to take over himself.

In consultation with his best man, the bridegroom

should appoint the necessary ushers — or 'groomsmen' as they are sometimes called. The number required will depend largely on the number of people who are invited to the church ceremony. If less than fifty or sixty guests are invited, then only two ushers are generally needed. A further two ushers could well be needed to cope with each additional fifty/sixty guests, though there is no hard and fast ruling on the matter. The need is to have sufficient ushers to receive the guests in the church porch and to conduct them to their places for the service.

When appointing the ushers the bridegroom and his best man have to take into account family 'considerations'. It is usual to make the choice from the unmarried brothers and friends of both the bridegroom and his bride and a great deal of tact needs to be exercised if somebody is not going to protest: 'If you ask *him*; you can't leave out *so-and-so*'.

It is important however that each side should be represented in order that as many as possible of the guests will be recognised and received by name. It is quite in order for an usher to meet a guest in the porch and ask, 'Friend of the bride; or of the groom?', in order to determine on which side of the church they should sit, but it is much more welcoming to receive them by name and, therefore, know the pew to which they should be conducted.

The correct seating arrangements are:

Parents, relatives and friends of the *bride* should be seated in the pews on the *left* of the nave facing the altar.

Parents, relatives and friends of the *bridegroom* should be seated in the pews on the *right* of the nave facing the altar.

In each case, parents, grandparents, brothers and sisters should occupy the front pews (leaving enough room for the groom and best man in the front right pew) and immediately behind them, other relatives followed by friends.

The ushers should seat themselves near the back in order to be in a convenient position to deal with any late-comers.

4

Duties

To ensure that the wedding runs smoothly, the best man needs to liaise closely with the chief bridesmaid.

In all probability the bride will come from the same circle of friends as her groom and they will choose their chief bridesmaid and best man from that group. In that event, it will be easy for the best man and chief bridesmaid to discuss the wedding arrangements together.

However, it may happen, of course, that the bride is a stranger to the best man, or that she has selected a chief bridesmaid who is unknown either to the groom or best man, or both. In such an event, it is a good idea if the bridegroom and bride invite the best man and chief bridesmaid out for a drink or a meal so that they can talk and get to know one another.

If the bride lives a considerable distance from the groom and best man, then it may be more difficult to arrange an evening out. In these circumstances, the groom could arrange for his best man to accompany him to his fiancée's home town so that they can meet the chief bridesmaid.

The best man has no official status in the advance arrangements being made for the engagement party, the stag party, the wedding or the reception — though, of course, he has important duties to perform at both the service and the reception afterwards.

The engagement party is entirely the affair of the bride and her future husband; the stag party is normally arranged by the bridegroom, perhaps with the assistance of his best man (though sometimes the best man may arrange it); the wedding is arranged by the bridegroom and his future wife in consultation with the incumbent of the church concerned — and the reception to follow is traditionally booked by the bride's parents (although nowadays the bride and groom may book it themselves).

Before the Wedding
The best man is concerned chiefly in seeing to it that the bridegroom is preparing himself for his wedding, so he is busy:

(a) Appointing the ushers in consultation with the bridegroom.

(b) Making sure of the degree of formality expected at the wedding and seeing to it that the bridegroom obtains the right clothing for the occasion. At the same time he will instruct the ushers accordingly and organise his own wedding clothes. If he is hiring his clothes, he will arrange to collect them the day before the wedding.

(c) Helping the bridegroom with the arrangements

for the stag party – if he is asked; and clearing up afterwards if necessary.

(d) Ordering a wedding car for himself and the bridegroom if one is required, and arranging another car for the newly-weds for their departure after the reception, if needed.

(e) Checking that the buttonholes for the bridegroom, best man and ushers have been included in the bride's order to the florist.

Hand over the wedding ring at the appropriate moment.

On the Morning of the Wedding

The best man must:

(a) Pick up the buttonholes for himself and the bridegroom, if they are not to be delivered.

(b) Dress in his full wedding outfit first so that he is free to attend the bridegroom from then on.

(c) Conduct the possibly nervous bridegroom to the church.

(d) Be the custodian of the wedding ring(s) until needed during the wedding ceremony.

(e) Take charge of the honeymoon documents and the bridegroom's luggage.

At the Church

The best man will:

(a) Take the bridegroom to his ordained place at the foot of the chancel steps.

(b) Hand over the wedding ring(s) at the appropriate moment during the service.

(c) Go to the vestry after the service, to sign the marriage register as a witness.

(d) Marshal the wedding party for the photographer at the church door.

(e) Usher the newly-weds into their car.

(f) Pay the marriage fees, if this has not been done.

After the Service

The best man must hurry to the venue of the reception

and:

(a) Help to marshal the guests towards the receiving line.

(b) Act as toast-master, unless a professional toast-master is employed.

(c) Reply to the toast of 'the bridesmaids'.

(d) Read out the telemessages of congratulations that have been received by the bridal couple.

(e) Return to the bridegroom the travel documents in connection with the honeymoon.

(f) See the couple — and their luggage — to their car or taxi. And aid their departure.

(g) Speed the parting guests and, if required, escort the bridesmaids to their homes.

(h) Collect the bridegroom's discarded wedding clothes and, if necessary, return them as soon as possible to the hire firm.

(i) Help to collect and transport the wedding presents to the home of the bride's parents, if needed.

5

What To Wear

Some weddings are more formal than others, and the type of clothing worn by the main participants depends on a number of factors: on whether the bride and groom have been married before; on their age (sometimes a less 'showy' ceremony is more appropriate for the marriage of a 'mature' couple); on the number of guests attending (sometimes the ceremony takes place at a great distance from the homes of the parties concerned and therefore few guests are present); on the lack of time between the decision to marry and the ceremony itself; and, of course, on financial circumstances.

The *formal* outfit for the bridegroom, the best man and the ushers is 'morning coat'. This is not commonly used these days. It comprises:

(a) Black morning coat.

(b) Grey striped trousers − without turn-ups.

(c) Grey waistcoat − usually double-breasted with lapels.

(d) Grey tie — the cravat is rarely worn today.

(e) White shirt — with a turn-down collar.

(f) Black socks and shoes.

(g) A white handkerchief in the breast pocket.

There are variations in fashion all over the world, and indeed from one part of Britain to another. A style that has become more fashionable is a grey morning suit (with tails). A cravat *is* sometimes worn with this, and grey socks and black shoes are worn. It is up to the bridegroom to conform to the style of the moment, and of the locality.

It is not, however, necessary for formal dress to be worn. A suit is just as acceptable nowadays.

Unless the wedding is almost a 'State occasion', the formality of dress does not apply to everyone present. Those who are expected to conform with the bridegroom (who sets the fashion) are:

(a) The best man who must support the bridegroom.

(b) The bride's father who will be in the forefront at his daughter's side.

(c) The ushers.

(d) The groom's father.

If the wedding is of the 'fashionable' degree, the following people should also be added to the list of those expected to dress in the same fashion as the bridegroom — though they need not do so if the wedding is of lesser interest to the general public:

(a) The bridegroom's brothers.

(b) The bride's brothers.

(c) Other close family relatives.

(d) Friends who happen to be well-known figures in the neighbourhood.

Other male guests may please themselves as to what they wear, but lounge suits are preferable.

Grey wedding 'toppers', though still worn, have become less often seen — though no other form of headgear may be worn with a morning coat at a wedding.

It is difficult to wear them in the modern, low-roofed car or taxi on the way to and from the church and the reception rooms; nor can they, of course, be worn indoors.

In fact the 'topper' can even be more of a nuisance than a decoration — and even a worry. Imagine having, after the service in the church, to find your top-hat from amongst a stack of others, all exactly similar and most of them bearing, as the only means of identification the same maker's label!

One chance of wearing a hat comes during the very few moments spent in getting into and out of cars, but the more important time is the period spent on photographs at the church door. Indeed, this is really the only reason for being burdened with a hat at all!

Needless to say, a less formal wedding is no less solemn nor less important to its participants than one staged in the height of fashion.

Even though the bride may wear her wedding gown with its train and veil, there is no reason why the interested parties should not agree on a more relaxed style for the men.

Different forms of dress:

Left: Formal – suitable for a 'posh' wedding.

Middle: Smart suit – suitable for most weddings.

Right: Donkey-jacket – not suitable for a wedding at all.

In such cases the bridegroom, his best man and indeed all male members of the wedding party, should be dressed in lounge suits. In full, the dress normally comprises:

(a) A lounge suit of the current style (usually light in colour).

(b) The waistcoat should be of the same material though this item is often omitted, especially in the spring and summer.

(c) The trousers should be of the same material — so that the suit in full is entirely suitable for normal wear instead of having to be put to one side after the wedding.

(d) Shirt with turn-down collar.

(e) Socks and shoes, in accordance with the rest of the attire.

(f) A handkerchief showing from the breast pocket, colour to blend with the suit.

(g) A tie, usually silk, to go with the suit.

The only other item of wear that should not be omitted for a wedding is the buttonhole. It is often a white carnation, but nowadays, it is quite in order for men to wear buttonholes that enhance their suits — so it might be a red rose, or a red, yellow or pink carnation. It has been known for a florist to provide a black buttonhole to go with an all-white suit! Very often the bridegroom, best man and the two fathers will have one colour buttonhole, and the ushers and any other male members of the wedding party another colour so that they can be easily identified especially if they are all wearing grey 'penguin' suits.

Other male guests may also like to provide buttonholes for themselves to wear.

One other worrying feature of the dress regulations concerning the male members of the wedding party can be the expense involved. It certainly seems a waste of money to buy a morning suit that will probably be worn only a very few times in a lifetime − possibly on a single occasion.

However, it is a simple matter today to hire the suit for the day for a relatively small amount of money − and it is now almost the universal practice to do so, even by the bridegroom and his best man.

There are many firms from whom you can hire suits. But it is important to make arrangements for their hire well in advance of the date they are actually required − if you are to obtain a first-class fit.

6

The Stag Party

Before the day of the wedding, the best man may find himself attending a number of parties connected with the event.

Some brides and grooms fight shy of too much ostentation in this direction, preferring to save their energies — and perhaps their finances — for the 'big' day. Others, perhaps more gregarious, hold all the traditional pre-wedding parties.

There will probably be the engagement party; a small get-together to introduce the best man and chief bridesmaid to one another (as mentioned on page 19); the family party where both sets of parents are brought together and which the best man and the chief bridesmaid may well be expected to attend. There may even be a 'we were all unmarried friends' affair — but *last* of them all as far as the bridegroom and his best man are concerned, is the stag party.

It is at this event the bridegroom entertains for the last time his male friends — a serio-comic affair, full of mock-nostalgia and high-spirited finality.

The origin of the custom of holding such a party appears to be lost somewhere deep amongst the mysterious wedding superstitions of old. The idea seems to have arisen as nothing more serious than the wish of a gathering of friends to say a mocking farewell to him amongst them who was about to sacrifice his freedom for the doubtful state of married bliss. A last fling before a bridegroom assumed the mantle of responsibility and comes under the sobering influence of a feminine partner — putting an end to the 'wild oats' period of his life.

The aftermath.

At one time the stag party was invariably scheduled for the eve of the wedding — sometimes with disastrous results.

By the very nature of the party and the fact that it is a 'men only' affair, it will almost certainly be a 'high-spirited' event — with the distinct possibility of a few 'hangovers' on the following morning.

As this is the morning of the wedding it can be a sad and anxious morning for a somewhat distraught bridegroom, an uneasy — and queasy — period for the best man and many of the guests who had attended the previous night's party — and most distressing to the bride.

In fact, particularly in the days of the Prince Regent — and often enough since — it was not unknown for a man to have to be conducted to the altar by a best man almost as unfit to stand up as the bridegroom himself; neither of them in a fit condition to follow the details of the service. And almost as often, in great-great-grand-father's time, the bridegroom would be forced by misguided friends to take the 'hair of the dog that bit him' before the wedding and at the reception afterwards, resulting in his bride finding herself tearfully alone on their wedding night, while her sadly inebriated husband sleeps stertorously and soundly through the night.

Fortunately, and possibly at the instigation of many an unhappy bride, it has now become the custom to hold the stag party some days in advance of the wedding — leaving plenty of time for recuperation before the great day.

It is the bridegroom's prerogative to invite only his own male friends to the stag party. As his best friend, of course, the best man will be the first to be asked. The others he can be expected to ask are his brothers

— and, if he is wise, his bride's brothers. The actual numbers will depend on the number of friends claimed by the groom — and his financial resources.

In the past it was the custom that all the guests be bachelors, but nowadays it is common for married friends and relatives to be invited. Of course, no females will be admitted under any circumstances.

In general practice the guests, though of the same generation as the bridegroom, should not be under the age of 17; 18 is a more realistic age, where possible, in view of the prohibitions laid down by the Liquor Licensing Laws.

Nowadays, the stag party will often consist of drinks at a local pub (or pubs) and be a very informal affair. Sometimes, it will include a meal. Occasionally it will be held in a private room in a pub or in a hotel; or it may even be staged in the bridegroom's home or that of his parents (in which event the parents will, of course, be expected to go out for the evening).

The main speech of the evening is expected to be made by the best man. If the evening includes a meal, then the best man will probably be sitting at the foot of the table and will make his speech at the coffee stage.

The speech should be entertaining, humorous, full of happy stories, and slanted to poke as much fun as possible at the bridegroom.

Unless he is extremely quick-witted with an unusually fast-moving mind, the best man should prepare in advance the text of his speech and, if necessary, rehearse it to the point where it sounds 'off the cuff' and unrehearsed.

The contents must be amusing, anecdotal and entirely concerned with the bridegroom and his friends. It must be of sufficient length, but not too long so that it starts to bore the listeners.

Points that may be used in such a speech include:

(a) Some amusing incidents of the bridegroom's childhood.

(b) The unfortunate girls that are now to be abandoned by the bridegroom — and the difficulties in getting rid of them.

(c) The idea that two can live as cheaply as one being a fallacy.

(d) Some of the means whereby he can escape his fate: the river, the French Foreign Legion, a Trappist Monastery, or a slow boat to the East.

The bridegroom's reply should be the only other speech of the evening — and if there is any entertainment to follow, it should be brought on at this stage.

An entertainment is not really necessary at such a party though it is occasionally added, particularly if there are any theatrical people present. Generally, by the time the speeches have been made — and sufficient alcohol consumed — the guests are able to make their own entertainment.

The host should be the last to leave the party — usually in company with his best man and, if necessary, by taxi. The best man should be in a fit state to make sure that anyone driving home from the party is fully sober.

7

The Wedding Eve

The day preceding the wedding is a busy one for all concerned — not least, for the best man. He is likely to be required to help the bridegroom in all sorts of unexpected directions — as often as not to soothe away some unnecessary worry — and to assist the bride in matters between herself and her husband. 'Has he remembered to...?', 'You haven't let him forget...?' and 'Do see to it that he...' are all growing symptoms of wedding day nerves.

Before he becomes too involved in personal problems posed by any and everybody associated with the wedding, it is well for the best man to check on the preparations for which he will be held responsible. He should leave nothing to chance and amongst the more important queries he should make are:

(a) Has the florist got the order for the buttonholes required by the bridegroom and himself? And as it is probable that the ushers and some of the male guests have asked for their buttonholes to be added to the order, check on them too.

(b) If hiring suits, collect them for both the bridegroom and himself.

(c) Make sure that all items of clothing, other than any hired suits, are already in his own wardrobe and that of the bridegroom, as well as shirts, socks, ties and clean handkerchiefs.

(d) That there has been no slip-up in the order for taxis − and their exact timetable. They may be wanted to carry the best man and the groom to the church, to convey the newly-weds from the church to the reception, with a second for taking the best man and the bridesmaids to the same place, and on occasion a third and fourth car will be needed to take both sets of parents, and any elderly relatives from the church to the reception. And if the bridal couple are to leave from the reception rooms for their honeymoon by taxi, an order must be placed for that too.

(e) That the bridegroom is in possession of the wedding ring(s).

(f) Has the bridegroom collected together the honeymoon documents? Check them to make sure that none has been forgotten. The best man will undoubtedly be blamed if the newly-weds arrive at Las Palmas − or wherever their destination is − to find that they have left behind their money and credit cards!

Depending on the honeymoon resort and the mode of travel, documents may well include credit cards or travellers' cheques, passports, rail, ferry and/or air tickets; hotel reservation confirmations and excursion tickets. As this list is by no means exhaustive, it would be well if the bridegroom got together with the best man and listed them well in advance — so that his last-minute check can be made with certainty.

(g) That the bridegroom has completed the main part of his packing for the honeymoon journey — leaving only, for the following morning, such things as last-minute toilet items and the clothing he intends to change into from his wedding outfit.

The best man should make an opportunity during the day to call on the bride's mother to collect the Order of Service sheets required for distribution in the church and should allow time for being roped in by the bride's family for various chores. By this time, the best man should have been in touch with each usher and told them roughly what their duties will be, and the time they should be at the church. He should arrange to meet the chief usher to hand over the Order of Service sheets with any other last-minute details, some time during the day. The chief usher will receive instructions whether to offer an Order of Service sheet to each guest as they enter the church and are escorted to their seats, or whether the sheets should be placed on each seat in the church before the guests arrive.

Guidance may have to be given as to the proper way to greet the guest and the correct places among the pews in which each should be seated.

The customary seating arrangements for the wedding guests are detailed on page 52.

Once the best man has dealt with the Order of Service sheets he may then offer his services to anyone else who needs them. This may involve transporting the cake from the bakers to the caterer at the reception, if the baker does not make his own deliveries; or taking the going-away luggage to the changing room at the hotel which is being used for the reception.

It may also involve taking the wedding presents to the reception rooms where they are to be displayed. This latter task may take quite a lot of time and require more than one journey between the bride's home and the reception.

Exhibition of wedding gifts.

The usual method of arranging the exhibition of wedding presents is to set up tables in a room set aside for the purpose; the number of tables depending, of course, on the number and size of the gifts.

The tables should be covered with white tablecloths and perhaps tiered with the aid of large boxes decorated with coloured paper — or, of course, the white tablecloths.

The presents usually need to be removed from their packages — though the cartons should be retained so that the items can be transported to the bride's home eventually, without damage.

Each gift should be identified by a white card, as often as not sent with it, set up beside the piece on the show tables. They should be inscribed with the donor's name and address, and perhaps the relationship of the giver to the bride or the bridegroom.

It is quite possible that a number of wedding presents take the form of a cheque. In such cases, (as with gifts of insurance policies, share certificates, or possibly the deeds of a flat or house) for safety's sake the cheques should be banked as soon as possible, and the certificates, etc., put in a safe place. For display purposes, the donors' names can be listed on a piece of card, but the amount should never be shown, i.e.:

Cheques have been received from:
  Mr. & Mrs. John Green and Alexandra
  Mr. & Mrs. Robert Walker
etc.

Someone should be held responsible for locking the door of the room where the presents are being displayed and safeguarding the key until the following day.

However, it may be better not to have the wedding

gifts on display in a hotel, or in a hall during the reception, as it may be difficult to guarantee their security. In that case, the gifts could be displayed at the home of the bride's mother and viewed by the wedding guests, perhaps at an evening party held directly after the wedding reception. Alternatively, the bride and groom might like to display the gifts in their new home. If so, they may like to send out cards (available from stationers) as follows:

> 10 Bow Road
> Horley
> Surrey
> RH1 7QL

Dear

We would like to express our sincere thanks for your kind wishes and lovely gift.

Would you please come to our Show of Presents on Wednesday 17th September at 7.30 p.m.

> Jane and Mark

The Church Rehearsal
The church rehearsal normally takes place some time during the week preceding the wedding; the most common and convenient day being the eve of the wedding as all the main participants will probably be staying in or near the bride's home town. It is very important that the best man attends the rehearsal, as should, of course, the groom, bride, bride's father, and bridesmaid(s). The clergyman who is conducting the wedding will run through the service with them so that they will all know exactly what their own individual role is during the ceremony.

8

The Wedding Morning

Whatever the scheduled time of the wedding, the best man must be up and about at an early hour. He will probably dress in utility clothes to save time while he gathers together the numerous items required by the bridegroom and himself — and not forgetting any commissions he has promised to undertake for the bride.

If he and the groom are not hiring a car or taxi but are driving themselves to the church, the best man should, at the very least, make sure that they have enough petrol to get to the church on time.

Probably the first call will be a hurried visit to the bridegroom's home to check that all is well, followed by a rush around to the bride's home to carry out any errands for her, and to collect the buttonholes.

Back to his own home to dress in his own wedding clothes and to ensure, in good time, that he has all the items required by a best man for the performance of his task.

Normally the wedding fees will have been paid in

advance, but if they have not, the best man should make sure he carries sufficient funds in his pocket to cover them.

The most frustrating part of a best man's duties at this stage, particularly if the bridegroom is inclined to be nervous and over-anxious, is to attend on him during

Pinning the buttonholes into place.

the last stages of his preparation for the ceremony.

The best man should have plenty of time in hand when he arrives at the home of the bridegroom, already fully dressed and ready for the journey to the church.

The first thing is to get the bridegroom into his

wedding outfit — leaving time to deal with any emergencies, caused by forgetfulness, that may arise: a missing button, a broken shoe-lace, a badly crumpled tie — any one of a hundred trivial items that can go adrift and mar the 'big' day.

If the bridegroom's mother is going to be asked to pin the buttonholes into place, the best man should remember that she and her family are due at the church early and so must leave home some time in advance.

As soon as he is satisfied that the bridegroom is properly dressed, the best man should check and take charge of the following items:

(a) The wedding ring(s) — which are best placed in a waistcoat pocket, deliberately selected so that the best man will not forget where he put them and have to start an undignified search of his pockets at the very moment he is due to place them on the Prayer Book, in the hands of the minister.

(b) The various documents required for the honeymoon, as gathered together on the previous day.

(c) After ensuring that the bridegroom has completed his packing for the journey, the best man should take temporary charge of the suitcases — and the keys.

(d) Make certain that the bridegroom packs all the clothing he will need to change into after the reception and for travelling. These must, of course, be packed separately — and again, placed in the care of the best man.

If the best man still finds himself with time in hand and is not likely to be delayed by traffic conditions, he should take the opportunity of running the suitcases to the scene of the reception and depositing them there ready for the departure of the newly-weds.

Perhaps a happier alternative to this is for the best man to persuade one of the ushers to collect the suitcases at the bridegroom's home and convey them to the reception room — so long as he leaves plenty of time to arrive at the church before the first of the guests.

A less reliable, though often practised method, is for the bridegroom and his best man to make a diversion on their way to the church, to deliver the cases. However, extra time must be allowed for traffic problems en route as they must make sure they arrive at the church in good time.

As soon as all these preparations are complete, the time arrives for the bridegroom and his best man to pace nervously about the room, waiting for the arrival of the taxi. The fact that it may not be due for another ten minutes will do little to ease the niggle of worry in their minds.

'I bet it's going to be late,' prophesies the bridegroom.

'It's the traffic that worries me,' sighs the best man. 'There's a football match on in town so there's sure to be a hold up.'

'You're sure you didn't forget to order it?'

'Of course I didn't — but that doesn't say you can rely on it getting back from some previous journey on time.'

'There could have been an accident.'

But despite all the doubts, it is more than probable that the driver will knock on your door within one minute of the time arranged. And as he is both an expert on the route and in forecasting the traffic flow, he will deposit the bridegroom and the best man at the door of the church right on time.

'On time' should mean fifteen to twenty minutes before the bride is due to arrive on the arm of her father – or if she has no father, of whoever is to give her away.

9

The Church of England Ceremony

Having arrived at the church on time, the bridegroom and his best man should find themselves some out-of-the-way spot where they can wait in peace until it is time for them to take their places. The clergyman often takes this opportunity to invite the bridegroom to check the details for the register, and this is a convenient time to settle any unpaid fees.

If the groom and best man are wearing hats and gloves, they should be placed conveniently for the best man to carry both his and the bridegroom's to the vestry after the service.

As soon as he has satisfied himself that the bridegroom is likely to remain undisturbed, the best man should give himself a few minutes to ensure that the ushers are receiving the wedding guests at the church door, conducting them to their pews and handing out the Order of Service sheets. He should make sure, and help if necessary, to break up any tendency on the part of the guests to stop and chat in the church porch, so holding up the seating of the congregation and blocking the entrance. This is especially important if the wedding is a large one.

It is always a temptation for guests and relatives, who may not have met for a long time, to greet one another fulsomely and at length.

'It must be all of twenty years,' says one.

'And how is your daughter? Anne, isn't it?'

'Annabel. She's fine, but didn't you hear? She's married. Has a fine baby boy of her own now.'

'Well, I never. And your own son, didn't he become an architect?'

'An archaeologist, as a matter of fact. His will be the next wedding, I expect. Such a nice girl. You probably remember her mother Jean Blake. Thompson, she was.'

And so on, and so on. And can you blame them?

Arrival of bridesmaids and page.

The bride and father process down the aisle.

A little tact will go a long way to persuade people to withhold their family reminiscences until the reception that is due to take place after the service.

The chief bridesmaid is due to arrive five minutes ahead of the bride — accompanied by the rest of the bridesmaids and, if there are any, the pages. The best man should not stay to talk to her but accept this as his signal to return to the bridegroom down a side aisle if available and to conduct him quietly and slowly to a seat in the front right hand side pew until the wedding procession arrives at the church door.

For the next two or three minutes the bridegroom will cast anxious glances over his shoulder towards the church door in search of his bride. 'Is she going to turn up?' no doubt will pass through his mind — while the best man nervously fingers the wedding rings to make sure — for the fiftieth time, no doubt — that they have not vanished.

This is the one time in her life that the bride is expected to arrive exactly on time. The bride who arrives early can cause great panic. If necessary, the driver must be instructed to make some detour so as to arrive on time. If she is late, apart from the slight to her waiting groom, it might well be interpreted as discourtesy by the clergyman, the officials and the guests.

Besides, and even more important, it is possible that another wedding is due to follow immediately afterwards — and a late start must mean a hurried, even garbled, service, or complete disorganisation for the other unhappy couple.

Suddenly, as the organist will have been warned of the arrival of the bride, the church will be filled with the first notes of one of the wedding marches and as the congregation stands, the bridegroom and best man should move towards the chancel steps where they will stand facing the altar. The bridegroom should leave room on his left for the bride who will arrive on her father's right arm. The best man should stand on the bridegroom's right.

The bridegroom and best man should turn to welcome the bride as she approaches in procession down the aisle. The bride, with her face shielded by her veil, should be looking towards the chancel steps and the waiting bridegroom and best man. The bridesmaids, led by the chief bridesmaid, follow her two by two. If there are any pages they are likely to be very young who may either march ahead of the bridesmaids — after the chief bridesmaid — or, if their attention is likely to wander, paired off with the bridesmaids.

As the bride reaches her groom's side, he and the best man should turn to face the clergyman who will, usually, move to his place as the procession approaches down the aisle.

As the bridal party comes to a standstill, the organ will fade out leaving silence for the clergyman. The chief bridesmaid should step forward as the bride's father frees his daughter's arm, take the bride's bouquet, lift the veil back from her face and adjust her train if necessary. She then returns to her place, usually behind the bride.

At this point there is commonly a hymn which allows everybody a chance to settle any last-minute nerves.

ASB (Alternative Service Book) 1980 provides for a prayer and Bible reading at this point if desired.

The clergyman then begins the ordained service by:

1.   Stating the reason for the gathering in the church.

2.   Stating the reason for matrimony.

3.   Demanding to know if there are any impediments to the marriage; first from the congregation and then from the bridal couple. (Any objector may be required to furnish a bond as an earnest of good faith.)

If no valid objections are voiced, the clergyman will then ask the bridegroom:

'Wilt thou have this Woman to thy wedded wife, to

live together according to God's law in the holy estate of Matrimony? Wilt thou love her, comfort her, honour and keep her in sickness and in health; and, forsaking all other, keep thee only unto her, so long as ye both shall live?'

The bridegroom answers: 'I will.'

The clergyman then asks the bride:

'Wilt thou have this Man to thy wedded husband, to live together according to God's law in the holy estate of Matrimony? Wilt thou love him, comfort him, honour and keep him in sickness and in health; and forsaking all other, keep thee only to him, so long as ye both shall live?'

The bride answers: 'I will.'

The clergyman will then ask:

'Who giveth this Woman to be married to this Man?'

The bride's father (or whoever is giving her away) should not, but very often does, answer: 'I do.'

The bride's father passes his daughter's right hand to the clergyman, palm downwards. The clergyman passes it into the right hand of the bridegroom.

The bride's father takes no further part in the service and he may now, if he so wishes, drop back and take his place in the front pew beside his wife — though more commonly, it is the practice to remain at his daughter's side until after the clergyman has pronounced the couple man and wife and given them a blessing. The important thing is that if he moves, it should be as unobtrusively as possible.

The bridegroom will now say after the clergyman,

Position as the bride's procession reaches the front of the aisle.

repeating phrase by phrase:

'I .... take thee, ... to my wedded wife, to have and to hold from this day forward, for better for worse, for richer for poorer, in sickness and in health, to love and to cherish, till death us do part; according to God's holy law, and thereto I give thee my troth.'

The pair will free their hands and then the bride will take the right hand of the bridegroom in her own right hand and say after the clergyman, repeating phrase by phrase:

'I .... take thee, ... to my wedded husband, to have and to hold from this day forward, for better for worse, for richer for poorer, in sickness and in health, to love and to cherish, till death us do part, according to God's holy law, and thereto I give thee my troth.'

As they free their hands, the best man takes the wedding ring from his pocket and places it on the open page of the Prayer Book proffered by the clergyman. After a prayer for the blessing of the ring the clergyman will offer the ring to the bridegroom who will take it and place it on the third finger of the bride's left hand.

Neither the engagement nor any other ring should be worn on that finger during the service — and, in fact, it is usual to wear no ring on the hand until the wedding ring has been placed there.

While the bridegroom holds the ring in place on the bride's finger, he will repeat after the clergyman:

'With this Ring I thee wed, with my body I thee

ALTAR

CHOIR STALLS

CHOIR STALLS

MINISTER

BRIDE   GROOM

BRIDE'S FATHER   BEST MAN

CHIEF BRIDESMAID

PEWS   PEWS

BRIDE'S   BRIDEGROOM'S

                BRIDESMAIDS

RELATIONS   RELATIONS

AND FRIENDS   AND FRIENDS

Positions during the ceremony.

honour, and all my worldly goods with thee I share: In the Name of the Father, and of the Son, and of the Holy Ghost. Amen.'

The best man places the ring on the prayer book.

It is common nowadays for the bride to give a ring to the bridegroom. When this is so, the best man places both rings on the Prayer Book and they are both blessed. The bride puts the ring on the bridegroom's finger after she herself has received the ring he is giving her, either silently or saying the above words together with the groom.

When the bridal couple first meet the clergyman to discuss their wedding arrangements, they will be offered a choice of wording for their marriage; they may decide to choose to use the wording given in this chapter, or to be married with the words of the 1662 Prayer Book, which includes the promise by the bride to obey the husband. Alternatively, they could choose The Alternative Service Book, 1980, Series 3. This has promises in more modern language either with or without the word 'obey'; includes words for the bride either after receiving the ring or on giving a ring to the bridegroom; and provision is made for a couple who are active members of the church to have the ceremony during a service of Holy Communion.

After the giving of the ring(s), the clergyman may give a short address. This is followed by the nuptial blessing, prayers and a psalm or hymn. The Alternative Service Book provides for prayers written or chosen by the couple in consultation with the clergyman.

The clergyman or verger then leads the way to the vestry or side chapel, followed by the newly-married couple, the best man (bringing his own hat and gloves as well as those of the bridegroom if these are being worn) and the chief bridesmaid (bringing the bride's bouquet). The parents of both the bride and groom usually follow into the vestry to watch the signing of the register.

In the vestry or side chapel the bride will sign the register using her maiden name for the last time — though legally she may choose whether or not to take her husband's name. Her husband adds his signature followed by the clergyman and the two witnesses selected for the purpose. The selection of the two witnesses should have been made some time in advance and usually comprises the best man and the chief bridesmaid, provided that they are not under the age of 18 years.

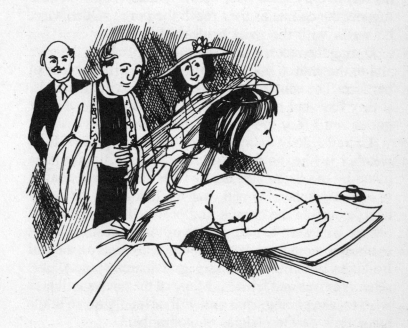

The bride signs the register.

As the guests will be waiting in the body of the church to see the bridal couple leave, only the briefest congratulations are in order in the vestry.

Again the organist will receive some secret signal, denoting that the bridal party is ready for the recessional, and will break into the appropriate march.

The bridegroom, with the bride on his left arm, will lead the way from the vestry or chapel followed by those present with them, in the same order as they entered. There is one exception to this where the layout permits — the best man will leave as early as he can and make his way to the church door by the quickest route, in time to meet the couple as they reach the porch. Otherwise, he walks with the chief bridesmaid.

During the recessional from the vestry, along the nave and to the church door, the bride's veil will be clear of her face. The couple may smile and nod to their friends, if they like, but must not pause or talk to any of their guests until they are beyond the church door.

There is likely to be some delay at this point. If the weather is fine, no doubt arrangements will have been made by the bride and her mother for the attendance of a photographer. He will wish to photograph the happy couple outside the church and beside the wedding car and he will want to add photos of the bridesmaids and the best man in attendance on them, as well as the full bridal party (mothers, fathers, grandparents, etc.), plus other relatives and friends. Many of the guests will also wish to take photographs and will normally do so at the same time as the official photographer.

As the unofficial master of ceremonies at this stage, the best man needs to keep a close watch on the time. The whole party will be due at the reception at some scheduled time and if the guests are late in arrival, they may find themselves reduced to having a cold meal and being rushed so that the newly-weds can catch a plane.

As soon as he can persuade the party and their guests to start moving, the best man must see the bridal couple

ALTAR

CHOIR STALLS

CHOIR STALLS

BRIDE'S FATHER   GROOM'S MOTHER

GROOM'S FATHER   BRIDE'S MOTHER

PEWS   PEWS

BRIDE'S   BRIDEGROOM'S

BRIDESMAIDS

RELATIONS   RELATIONS

AND FRIENDS   AND FRIENDS

GROOM   BRIDE

The recession after the service.

Photography.

to their car. It is at this point that confetti or rice is normally thrown at the bridal couple. However, if the clergyman requested at the beginning of the service that confetti should not be used as it causes litter, the guests should, of course, refrain from using it.

The best man should check that the bride has received the marriage certificate from the clergyman. If she has not, he should collect it. If it is not convenient for her to take it from him before she leaves for her honeymoon, the best man should hand it over to the bride's mother for safe keeping.

The bride and groom are expected to leave the precincts of the church first — followed by other cars carrying their parents, bridesmaids, family and then the guests. The best man and the ushers should make sure that everyone has transport for the journey to the reception.

Before he leaves the church, the best man should take the opportunity to ensure that the bridegroom's expenses have been settled, i.e. the marriage fee; the clergyman's fee, the organist's fee; and not forgetting the verger. Normally, these fees will have been paid in advance, but if they have not, then it is usually convenient for the best man to settle these accounts through the verger — the fee for the clergyman being handed over in a sealed envelope at the same time.

The best man should then hurry along to the reception where he will be needed. It is as well for him either to have his own car immediately available or a pre-ordered taxi standing by.

The Wedding of a Widow

Where the bride happens to be a widow, the wedding itself takes precisely the same form as that for a 'first' marriage, though it is traditional to expect less formality and the omission of much of the pageantry.

It is usual, though by no means obligatory, for the bride to forgo the bridal gown and the veil. Nor is she usually attended by bridesmaids, as the chief bridesmaid is replaced by a 'dame (or matron) of honour'. The order of selection is a (perhaps married) sister of the bride as the first choice, failing which a sister of the bride-groom is chosen or, if he has no sister or she would rather not be matron-of-honour, a close friend of the bride.

In deference to the bride's less formal attire, the bridegroom and his best man will usually wear 'lounge' suits, as will the ushers, if any are appointed.

The bridal bouquet and the buttonholes for the men are still customary.

It is usual for the matron-of-honour to join the bridegroom and the best man at their ordained place at the foot of the chancel steps, to await the arrival of the bride on her father's arm or that of another male relative. If the bride prefers, she need not process down the aisle, but instead may arrive at the church early with her father or other male relative and sit in a front-row pew until the time comes for her to step forward to the side of her bridegroom.

The number of guests invited to the wedding and the reception afterwards is a matter for the bride and her groom, though the time that has elapsed since the death of the bride's previous husband must be taken into consideration when the decision is made. If:

(a) The bride has been a widow for less than a year, the custom is to invite the parents of both parties to the wedding, a best man and a matron-of-honour. Invitations to friends should be restricted to only those who are close — the actual number being fewer and fewer, the shorter the period of widowhood. If, for some reason, the wedding takes place within a matter of weeks of the death of her previous husband, the invitations should be strictly limited to whoever is to give the bride away, a matron-of-honour, the best man and at the most, four to six friends or relatives.

(b) The generally accepted mourning period for a wife is considered to be a full year — and if this period has elapsed before her 'second' wedding is due to take place, no limitations are placed on the number of guests who may be invited both to the service and the reception afterwards — though the pageantry of the actual ceremony is still restricted to a less formal affair than for a 'first' wedding.

Whatever the bride decides to wear for her wedding, 'white' is considered to be suitable only for a 'first' marriage and is out of place for a widow.

The Wedding of a Widower

A widower is subject to far fewer restrictions when he marries for the second time, than is a widow. Though it is customary to restrict the pageantry usually associated with a first wedding, the style and scale of the event may be left to the bride and her parents. After all, it may be her first wedding; if so, she has the right to wear a bridal gown and a veil and be followed to the altar by bridesmaids — if she should so wish. As long as the bridegroom's first wife has been dead for more than a year, the bride may have the full panoply of the occasion.

If the couple intend to marry within a year of the first wife's death, then it would be better if the wedding was a low-key affair. Depending on the circumstances, it might be more appropriate if the bride were to postpone the wedding until after the full year.

Procession for a double wedding of two sisters.

A Double Wedding
The marriage of two couples at the same service before
the same clergyman, at the same time, and as part of
a single ceremony, is rather uncommon. The usual
reason for such an event is the desire of two sisters —
or occasionally brothers — to be married at the same
time.

Triple weddings occur at less frequent intervals, for
similar reasons, and it has been known for larger groups
to be married in a 'mass' wedding before a vast

'congregation', generally with some political or 'cult' motivation behind it.

The wedding of two or more couples at the same service may well be, and usually is, attended by the full formality and pageantry associated with such an occasion. Each bridegroom will be supported by his own best man, and each of the brides by her quota of bridesmaids. Each best man will undertake precisely the same duties on behalf of 'his' bridegroom as if the wedding was to consist of but a single bridal couple — though he may well find the need for conferences with the other best man (or 'men') to ensure that the whole affair runs cohesively and in harmony.

Orders of precedence become necessary where double — or multiple — weddings take place and the long-established rules are:

(a) The elder bridegroom is assumed to be the senior — without regard to the possible claims of the supporting families, or to the unlikely objections of one or both of the brides.

(b) In the procession, the brides' father would walk up the centre of the aisle with the senior bride (that is, the daughter who is to marry the elder bridegroom) on his right arm, and the junior bride on his left arm. Each bride would have her own bridesmaid(s) behind her.

If the brides are not sisters, then each party in the procession should be complete in itself. The bride of the senior bridegroom advances down the aisle on the arm of her father first, followed by her bridesmaids and pages. A few paces behind comes the second bride on *her* father's arm, with her own retinue of bridesmaids.

(c) The senior bridegroom and his bride take their vows first.

(d) The actual positioning of all the participants during the service will vary according to the architecture of the church, the space available, the width of the aisle, and the views and ideas of the clergyman (whose experience of previous double weddings is likely to be extremely limited!). The most important thing is that the brides' father gives the right girl to the right man! Adequate rehearsal is essential.

(e) The move to the vestry after the service should be led by the clergyman followed by the senior bridegroom and his bride — and those who are to accompany them there to sign, or witness the signing of the register. The junior bridegroom, his bride and his entourage follow next until both parties are in the vestry.

(f) The senior couple sign the register first, followed by their witnesses. Then follow the junior couple and their witnesses.

The two best men take an opportunity to leave the vestry as soon as possible and make their way as quickly as they can to the church door where they are responsible, jointly, for manoeuvring the two wedding parties, separately and together, before the photographers — and thereafter to the cars.

(g) In the recession each party should again be

complete in itself — the senior bridegroom, his bride and their attendants and relatives lead the way down the aisle and to the church door, separated by only a few paces from the second couple and their supporters.

Each best man should endeavour to see his 'own' bridal couple and their family and friends into their cars *en route* for the reception rooms — but it is quite in order for one to assist the other if it will help to get the cars away quickly, particularly if it is a wet day when the cars can draw up at the door only one at a time.

Where the duties of the two best men happen to clash, he who is in attendance on the senior bridegroom assumes the right of priority. This position of leadership is normally exercised at the reception where a single receiving line will be enough if the brides (or the bridegrooms) are relatives and are, in consequence, supported by the same parents.

Though it is possible for the two best men to take it in turns to marshal the reception guests past the receiving line, it is not possible for both to reply to the toast 'the bridesmaids' — unless the speeches are to go on interminably and become a series of repetitions. It is usual for the senior best man to undertake this duty — and, perhaps, delegate the post of toast-master to the junior best man.

This is a matter, however, for the senior best man to decide. He may well feel that his colleague is a better speaker than himself and reverse the accepted procedure.

Divorced People
The Church of England does not permit the remarriage

of *divorced persons*. This restriction is equally applicable where the marriage is concerned with either two divorced persons, or the marriage of a divorced man or woman to a single person. A clergyman could perform a marriage of divorced persons, but only if he and his bishop felt it would be right to do so. It is more common for a church service of blessing to follow a civil ceremony.

The Civil Law in Britain, however, does recognise the remarriage of divorced persons — in fact, if there are no other legal objections and the statutory requirements are carried out, a Superintendent Registrar may not refuse to conduct such a ceremony, though it will probably have to take place in a register office. For details of civil weddings, see page 79.

10

Ceremonies for Other Denominations & Civil Marriages

Of course, many people are not married under the Church of England and so in this chapter I give brief details of some other wedding ceremonies. The details of the best man's duties vary but little from church to church and can be accepted as standard — except where otherwise stated in this chapter.

The Roman Catholic Church
There are two different types of marriage service within the rites of the Roman Catholic faith. The 'Marriage celebrated during Mass' and the 'Marriage celebrated outside Mass'.

The 'Marriage celebrated during Mass' is much more elaborate, though the duties of the best man vary little from that expected in a 'Marriage celebrated outside Mass'. In each ceremony the first part is almost identical. This consists of an Entrance Rite, a Service of The Word, and the Rite of Marriage. Where the Mass is to be celebrated, the Liturgy of the Eucharist follows.

Two forms of the Entrance Rite are possible. In the first, the best man and the bridesmaids, along with the groom await the arrival of the bride at the door of the church. The priest greets the bride and groom at the church door, and a procession to the altar follows with the servers and the priest going first, followed by the bride and groom, best man and bridesmaids(s) and the parents. In a more traditional form of entry, the best man is standing at the groom's right hand in the place designated for them, usually the first pew on the right-hand side of the church. They await the arrival of the bride, who processes through the church with her father.

The Liturgy of the Word is mainly concerned with up to three readings from the Scriptures, after which the priest may deliver a homily. The Rite of Marriage follows. The arrangements for the marriage ceremony vary from place to place, according to the arrangements of the church furniture. Usually at this stage the bride and groom stand together in front of the priest. The best man stands on the right of the groom; he should make sure that he has the wedding ring, or rings, with him. After the exchange of vows and when the priest has said: 'What God has joined together, let no man put asunder', the blessing and exchange of rings follows. The normal custom is for the best man to place the ring(s) on a silver dish where it is blessed by the priest. The husband then places the ring on the wife's finger, and if the husband is to receive a ring, the wife places it on his finger. Bidding prayers follow, after which the couple, together with the witnesses, sign the civil register. This may be done in the church, or in the sacristy. Almost invariably, although it is by no means obligatory, the best man and the chief bridesmaid are appointed by the bridal couple as the official witnesses.

When the register has been signed, the ceremony either concludes with a final blessing, or the Nuptial Mass may follow. If this is the case, the best man and bridesmaids retire to the pews where they began the ceremony. At the end of the Mass the recessional begins. The bride moves down the aisle on the arm of her husband, and the best man and chief bridesmaid take their place immediately behind. They should be followed in their turn by the bridesmaids in pairs. Behind them, the father of the bride should escort the bridegroom's mother and the bride's mother should accompany the bridegroom's father. Bringing up the rear, the brothers and sisters of the bridal couple should follow in a similar manner to that of their parents.

On reaching the church door, the best man will assume the mantle of marshal — for the wedding photographs and the departures for the scene of the reception that is to follow.

There are certain other requirements which are no direct concern of the best man, but it is well that he should be aware of them as his advice may be sought.

1. A marriage inside the Mass is permitted in all cases except where one of the parties is not baptised.

2. A marriage between a Catholic and a baptised non-Catholic requires express permission from the Catholic party's parish priest.

3. A marriage between a Catholic and a non-baptised person needs a dispensation, obtainable through the parish priest.

4. The Catholic party has to undertake to avoid the danger of falling away from the faith, and sincerely to promise to do everything possible "within the unity of the partnership" to ensure the Catholic baptism and upbringing of all children of the marriage.

5. The priest must be able to sign a statement saying that in his opinion the non-Catholic will not oppose the fulfilment of the promise made by the Catholic.

6. Both parties will usually be asked to attend some form of marriage preparation. This will cover a variety of topics, some of these specifically concerning the essential qualities of Christian marriage, and some more general.

7. The wedding will normally take place in a Catholic church, but for good reasons a dispensation can be granted from this.

Although the marriage of *divorced persons* is normally refused in the Catholic Church, there may be instances where a previous marriage, for some reason, is not recognised by the Church. In these cases, a church marriage would normally be permitted. Such cases would exist when a declaration of nullity of the previous marriage had been granted to one of the persons by the Catholic Church, or if a previous marriage had not complied with Church Law.

In any event, the priest who is to conduct the service should be consulted well in advance by the couple for their own benefit, as if there are any 'snags' to be ironed out, this will give them plenty of time to get them organised. This applies particularly in the case of a 'mixed marriage', where one of the bridal couple is a non-Catholic. In this case, the priest should be consulted several months before the proposed wedding day.

The Free Churches

Though the Free Churches vary considerably in style, their marriage services are basically similar. They are likely to be simpler than those of the Church of England, but have the same intention and purpose.

A best man needs no special briefing in order to be able to perform his duties satisfactorily — so long as he follows the precepts laid down in this book. As with the Church of England, most Free Church ministers like to have a rehearsal of the ceremony, and the presence of the best man is important. His pre-wedding encouragement for the bridegroom, his duties during the service and his leadership during the celebrations afterwards follow the same pattern as is customary where the marriage is to take place within the rites of the Church of England. Many Free Churches do not have a centre aisle so everybody concerned should check which aisle is going to be used by the main participants for entering and leaving the church.

Also, it is a wise precaution to check with the bridal couple the minor details of the service peculiar to their church. The degree of formality varies somewhat from church to church which may be reflected in the celebrations afterwards. For example, alcohol may not be served at the wedding breakfast, and the speeches may have a more serious tone.

Quakers (Religious Society of Friends)

A Quaker wedding is a most solemn and, at the same time, a simple service. There is no pageantry, no ceremonial, no attendants, no music and no set sermon. In fact there is no public religious service — and no wedding ring.

The marriage is unique to the Society of Friends and consists mainly of silent, corporate worship. There is no preacher, no leader and no set procedure. The gathering is usually held in a Quaker Meeting House, made up of friends, relatives and even strangers. There is seldom a best man or a bridesmaid and the dress is wholly informal.

Only those who feel moved by the Spirit will rise to speak or kneel to pray.

At some point during the meeting, the bridegroom and bride take one another's hands and they will rise together, to their feet. Then the bridegroom will make his declaration:

'Friends, I take this my friend .... to be my wife, promising, through Divine assistance, to be unto her a loving and faithful husband so long as we both on earth shall live.'

The bride makes her own declarations in similar terms — then the wedding certificate is signed by the bridal couple in front of the Registering Officer. Two witnesses add their names and then the Registering Officer reads aloud the certificate. Afterwards, it is common practice for all others present at the meeting to append their signatures to the document.

Though there is no official place for the wedding ring

during the marriage rites, it is the custom for the couple to exchange rings afterwards.

It is usual at the close of the meeting for the couple to withdraw with full witnesses and the Registering Officer to complete the civil marriage register.

The Jewish Wedding

The Civil Law requires that all marriages take place before a Superintendent Registrar of Marriages and where Jews are concerned a marriage can be held in advance of the religious service or take place at the synagogue straight after the religious service. This is possible where the synagogue's Minister or secretary is recognised as the Registrar's representative by being a Secretary for Marriages.

A marriage under Jewish rites may only take place between two Jews − and they must be able to provide documentation to prove this, such as for example, that their parents were married in accordance with the Jewish rites themselves.

Though it is not absolutely obligatory for the best man to be of the same faith as the bridegroom, it is a rare occasion if he is not.

Generally, however, the best man is chosen from amongst the bridegroom's brothers, the senior having priority. Failing this, it is quite common for the selection to be made from amongst the bride's brothers. When neither the bridegroom nor his bride have brothers, the best man would then be chosen from amongst friends, but even then, it is usual to nominate a relative.

In any event, the duties of a best man are almost lost in the assistance given by the male relatives of both the bridegroom and the bride. The bridegroom is even escorted to his place under the canopy, where the wedding is solemnized, by his father, his bride's father and other male relatives of the two families.

The same escort then returns to the door of the synagogue — or wherever the ceremony is taking place — to meet the bride and to conduct her to her place at the side of her betrothed, under the canopy — on his *right*.

The details of the service vary between the orthodox synagogues, the more liberal and the reform communities, but in general the 'advisers' and 'attendants' on the bridegroom should be aware of the following customs and restrictions:

(a) The religious service may take place at any time of the day, on any day of the week, with the exception of Saturday; certain days of festival or mourning are also barred.

(b) On the Sabbath preceding the wedding, the bridal couple, accompanied by the father of each of them, should attend divine service. During the service, the bridegroom and close relatives will be honoured by being called upon to read passages from the Scroll of the Law.

(c) As well as her wedding dress, the bride wears a veil during the ceremony, together with long sleeves and gloves.

Everybody present, including the male members of the party, must have their heads covered.

Etiquette at the synagogue can vary. However, the groom is always expected to arrive first. Usually he sits in the Warden's box with his father, future father-in-law and best man.

The groom takes his place first under the *chuppah* (wedding canopy). The best man stands behind and to his left, with the ring handy.

The bride is generally brought in by her father, followed by bridesmaids, bride's mother with escort (or male relative), and bridegroom's parents. According to old Jewish custom, however, the bride is brought in by her mother and future mother-in-law. Both sets of parents usually stand beneath the *chuppah*.

Before the bride comes under the *chuppah*, however, the groom is formally requested by the Minister to approve the appointment of two witnesses of the *ketubah* (marriage document) and accept the terms and conditions of the *ketubah* whereby he undertakes a number of obligations to his wife.

The bride stands under the *chuppah* at the groom's right. At each side of the *chuppah* stand close relatives such as the couple's parents.

Next come the blessings of Betrothal, recited over a cup of wine. The first blessing is for wine and the second praises God for commanding us concerning forbidden marriages.

In Jewish law, the couple become married when the man places the ring on the woman's finger, with her acceptance signifying consent. It is important to note that this act effecting their union is carried out by the parties themselves, and it is not the Minister who 'marries' them, but they who marry each other, and the Minister's presence is as an expert in Jewish law, and sometimes as witness to the *ketubah*, as well as in a civil capacity if he is Secretary for Marriages.

Since the ring has such importance, it must be the

groom's property; should be of precious metal, but without jewels, and the bride should wear no other ring or jewellery during the ceremony. The ring is placed on the bride's right index finger, but she may transfer it to the 'ring finger' later. The reason for Jewish insistence on a plain ring is to allow no difference between rich and poor, and to avoid any deception or misunderstanding as to its value. It is placed on the right index finger because in ancient transactions this finger was used symbolically to acquire things.

The groom recites in Hebrew a declaration 'Behold, thou art consecrated unto me by this ring according to the law of Moses and of Israel', implying that both parties are properly married in accordance with Jewish law.

The *ketubah* is now read in Aramaic original and in English abstract and handed to the bride. She should look after it carefully since it is her interests which it recognises, and should it be lost she should get it replaced.

Then follow the seven blessings of marriage, with the final words of prayer that the bride and groom might find the perfect happiness of Adam and Eve and live a life of 'joy and gladness, mirth and exultation, pleasure and delight, love and brotherhood, peace and companionship'. At the conclusion of the Betrothal and the marriage blessings, the couple sip wine to symbolise the fact that they must share the same cup of life whether it be sweet or otherwise. This is followed by the breaking of a glass by the groom.

The ceremony concludes with the Minister pronouncing the blessing, in the heartfelt wish that its words of blessing, protection, grace and peace be fulfilled for bride and groom.

The couple sign the marriage documents, the bride signing her maiden name. The group leave the synagogue in procession with their attendants. Before greeting their guests at the reception they should spend a few minutes together in private (*yihud*), denoting their newly-acquired status as husband and wife entitled to live together under the same roof.

Civil Marriages

Nowadays more and more people are choosing to marry in a district register office in front of a Superintendent Registrar. There are many reasons for this — perhaps because the couple have no religious beliefs, or perhaps one or both of the parties is divorced, or perhaps for other reasons.

A civil marriage is a much simpler affair than a church wedding and, of course, includes no religious service. It normally lasts about five to ten minutes. However, register offices are able to provide flowers for the decorations and there is usually a waiting room so that guests can assemble and wait in comfort.

As with all weddings in the United Kingdom, the couple must each declare in turn in the presence of one another and before at least two witnesses that they are free to marry:

'I do solemnly declare that I know not of any lawful impediment why I ...... may not be joined in matrimony to ......'

Following this, they make a contract to join each other as man and wife:

'I call upon these persons here present to witness that I ...... do take thee ...... to be my lawful wedded husband/wife'.

The above words are written in the 1949 Marriage Act and may not be varied.

Many couples like to exchange rings and this can be part of the civil ceremony if wished.

The best man takes no formal part in the proceedings, but, as with church weddings, he is usually chosen as one of the witnesses to the marriage and so is required to sign the register.

11

The Reception

Pre-Reception Arrangements
The parents of the bride are the traditional hosts at the reception following the wedding ceremony. It is they who decide whether to have the reception at home, in a marquee in the garden, in a suitable local hall or at a local hotel. They will decide on the menu and the wines, order the wedding cake, arrange for the decorations and any other facilities such as a changing room for the bride. It is they who send out the invitations — after consulting the bridegroom concerning his wishes in the matter.

Traditionally, the bride's parents pay for the entire wedding reception and so they naturally decide the scale of the reception, the numbers to be invited and the quality and style of the meal. However, nowadays with rising costs, it is quite usual for the bridegroom's parents to offer to pay for part of the reception; for example, for the drinks, or for an evening party after the reception. Indeed, with more and more couples choosing to marry later in life and so having more money at their disposal (perhaps more than their parents), it is quite in order for them to pay for the reception themselves if they so wish.

So that the best man can help the reception run smoothly, he will need to know the following information:

(a) The premises where the reception is to be held — and the facilities it will afford, such as changing rooms and the place where the receiving line can most conveniently be established.

(b) The number of guests to be expected with special references to any V.I.P.s who may be expected to attend.

(c) The expected time of arrival of the guests — and the bridal couple.

(d) If photographs are to be taken in the reception rooms — before the reception (perhaps outside in the hotel's gardens?), during it, and the cutting of the cake.

(e) The time set for the meal. (Is it hot or cold? Obviously promptness is of importance; essential if it is to be a hot meal.)

(f) Arrangements made for the receipt and collection of any telemessages, if the caterer is not to place them on the table beside the wedding cake.

(g) The seating plan — if there is one — and where it is to be shown for the convenience of guests.

(h) Who the speakers are to be. The best man should make careful enquiries to ensure that the speakers will not rise until they are called upon, that they do not duplicate each other's material, and that there are not too many of them! After all, the bridal couple will have a departure time to keep to.

(i) The time the couple must depart to catch their plane/train/ferry for the start of their honeymoon.

And he will want to know after the departure of the newly-weds and their guests:

(a) who will be expected to collect the remains of the wedding cake and take it to the home of the bride's mother, and;

(b) who is responsible for gathering together, packing and transporting to the home of the bride's mother, the collection of wedding presents if they have been on display.

Reception Venues

It is quite usual for a reception to be held at the home of the bride's parents. Generally, most homes have neither the space nor the kitchen facilities to cope with meals for more than a very limited number of guests. A popular solution is to hire a marquee to put in the garden, often connected to the house by an awning (in case of rain), and to engage the services of a caterer, who will prepare a meal, serve it and the drinks, and clear up at the end of the day, thus saving the bride's parents a great deal of extra worry.

At such a reception, the menu could be a cold buffet and include such items as plaice in orange sauce with anchovies, crab mayonnaise, chicken with grapes and

The marquee is a popular solution.

almonds, roast fillet of beef, gammon with pineapple, avocado mousse, terrine of duck with bacon, or salmon and cucumber flan served with a large variety of salads, followed by a choice of exotic sweets. All these items can be specially prepared as fork buffet food so that the bride and groom can circulate among friends and relatives, and they too can move around instead of being confined to one place. However, many people prefer to be able to sit down at such a buffet meal, as sometimes it can be difficult trying to eat from a plate of food in one hand while the other hand is holding onto a glass of wine! Therefore, a good host will make certain that there are enough chairs and tables so that every guest can sit if they wish to.

Modern marquees come in various widths and can be made up in any length. They can have coloured linings, wood floors, platforms, dance floors and matting to cover them, and can include chandeliers, spot and flood lighting if required. The firms who provide the marquees can also provide a large range of chairs and tables, from the elegant to the functional and will also provide heaters according to the season.

If the bride's parents decide on a marquee, they will often use it to hold a dance or disco during the evening for the newly-weds and any guests who may not have been invited to the reception.

There are many firms available today that specialise in wedding receptions and supplying accommodation and meals to suit all purposes — and purses. A hotel is often ideal — it can provide changing rooms for the bride, and if required, for the bridegroom; reception facilities apart from the restaurant; probably a separate room for the display of the wedding presents if required; and, of course, overnight accommodation for those guests who may have travelled some distance to the wedding.

Village or church halls are also popular venues for wedding receptions. At these halls, outside caterers are usually employed to provide the food and perhaps any decoration of the premises.

The reception line.

At the Reception
At the reception, in the few minutes before the guests arrive, it is usual for the formal photographs of the cutting of the cake to be taken by the official photographer.

The principals will then normally form a reception line to receive the guests. The guests will first meet the bride's mother and father (as the hosts), followed by the bridegroom's parents and then the bride and bridegroom. Alternatively, it can be the bride's parents, followed by bride and groom, followed by bridegroom's parents. The bridesmaids will stand at the end of the line to greet the guests.

The best man can direct the guests towards the bride's parents himself, or in some cases, there may be a Master of Ceremonies who will ask the guests' names and announce them before they go in to meet their hosts officially. The ushers should help to marshal the guests on their way to the receiving line.

The bride should never be congratulated on her marriage; she should be offered best wishes for her happiness!

The best man will need to encourage the guests to move on past the reception line as quickly as possible, otherwise there is likely to be considerable delay if fulsome guests are allowed to monopolise the newly-weds. This is most important at larger weddings where the queue of guests can become so long that they stretch outside — sometimes into the rain!

The best man should keep an eye on the time so that everything runs smoothly and without haste right up to the departure of the bride and bridegroom (which should be at a pre-arranged time). They will, of course, want to talk to their guests and this is much easier to do during a buffet reception than at the end of a more formal, sit-down meal, when there is little time left before leaving the reception.

Having passed along the reception line, the guests will then be offered a drink — perhaps sparkling wine, sherry, champagne, apple juice or grape juice — and there will probably be nuts and other titbits to nibble.

At very formal receptions, a toast-master will call the guests to their seats. At buffet receptions, it is more usual for the bride and groom, having received their guests to approach the buffet tables in order to be served first, which is the signal for others to follow.

Sometimes most, if not all, of the official photographs are taken at the reception itself rather than at the church. This may be because it is unfortunately raining and so the photos must be taken indoors, or because the gardens at the reception are more attractive than those at the church or register office, or perhaps because the wedding is taking place on a late winter afternoon when it is dark outside. In these circumstances, the guests will be presented with their drinks on arrival at the reception. The wedding photographs will then be taken, and afterwards the receiving line will be organised so that the guests officially meet the newly-weds, their parents and bridesmaids immediately before entering the dining area for the meal.

If the Wedding Breakfast is to be a sit-down meal, there should be a large seating plan near the door for the convenience of the guests, but the best man should have a general idea of the arrangements in advance. He should, in any event, know the exact placings at the top table.

As soon as the majority have begun to find their seats, the best man would be well advised to show the bridesmaids to their places and leave the still-waiting guests to be guided by the ushers.

Seating arrangements are very much a matter for the hostess, with the advice of the caterer, although she almost invariably consults her daughter who in turn

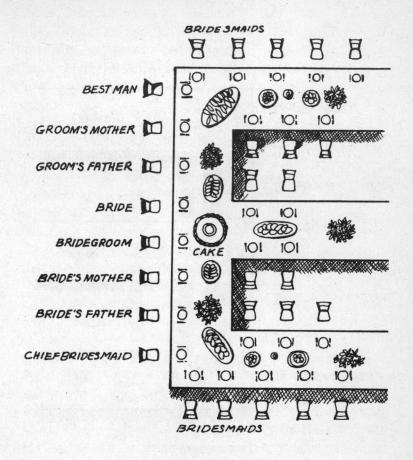

A typical seating layout.

seeks the advice of the bridegroom who probably asks the best man for his ideas on the subject.

The number of guests to be seated at the top table depends largely on the total number who are to be invited, and on the shape and layout of the room concerned.

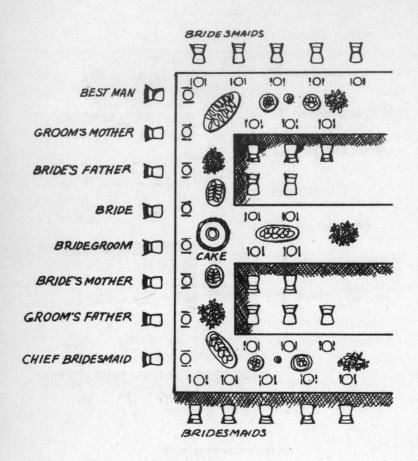

An alternative seating layout.

As it is usual for the bride and bridegroom to be seated together in the middle of this table, it must seat an even number of people. And only one side of the table should have places — so that the bridal couple may have an unimpeded view of their guests, and more important, the guests be able to see the principals.

The most common method of arranging a top table is that shown on page 89 but other suggestions such as those contained on page 90 and below are sometimes preferred and equally acceptable.

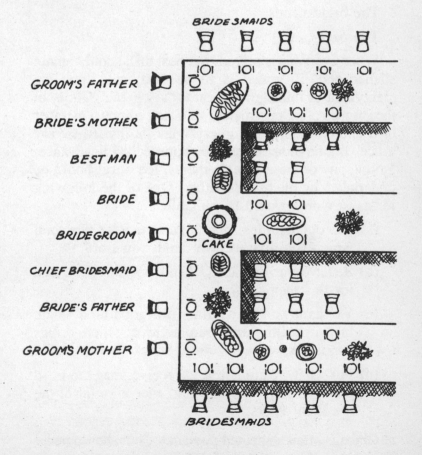

Another possibility.

As soon as the guests have found their seats, the bridal couple should move towards their places at the top table, together. They should be followed by:

The bride's father with the bridegroom's mother.

The bridegroom's father with the bride's mother.

The best man with the chief bridesmaid.

The bridesmaids.

The pages.

When everyone is seated, the best man should obtain silence and, if 'grace' is to be said, call upon the clergyman or minister present to 'say grace'. Often, in the absence of a clergyman or minister, a known member of a church among the guests may be invited to 'say grace'. But he or she should be approached in advance. Failing any of these arrangements, the duty should be undertaken by the bride's father. One of the following forms of words would be suitable:

(a) For our families, our friends and for this food which you give us, we thank you Lord.

(b) Receive our thanks, O Lord, for this food and for this happy day.

(c) We thank you, our Father, for good food which brings health, and human love which brings happiness.

(d) For what we are about to receive, may the Lord make us truly thankful and ever mindful of the needs of others.

Grace is often neglected nowadays, but should never be omitted if a minister of religion is present.

Cutting the cake.

The Cutting of the Cake

The cutting of the cake either takes place directly after the meal (just before the coffee is brought round), or immediately after the speeches. It is perhaps easier if it occurs before the speeches, as the cake can then be taken away to be cut up by the caterer, before being brought back and given to the guests. The guests are then able to eat it while listening to the speeches.

At whatever stage during the reception it takes place, it is the best man who should ask for order and announce that it is time for the cutting of the cake.

The bridegroom should then lead his bride to the most convenient place beside the cake — usually on the opposite side of the table to where they have been sitting. The caterer or one of his staff will be in attendance and he will assist the bride to place the point of the knife in the proper place near the middle of the bottom tier of the cake — and with the cutting edge towards her.

The bridegroom should then place his hand over that of his wife and slowly and carefully help her to push the point of the blade into the heart of the cake and then to draw it forward and downwards in a slicing movement.

That usually completes the token 'cutting of the cake'. The bride and her groom are not expected to undertake the laborious task of dividing the cake; this is a task to be undertaken by the caterer who will also pass the portions around on plates, sometimes with the assistance of the bridesmaids.

It is the caterer's job to dismantle the cake as he cuts it and set aside a considerable portion from which the bride, or her mother, will send small boxed pieces to those of their friends, relatives and acquaintances who have been unable to attend the wedding and the reception afterwards.

It used to be traditional for the bridesmaids to keep their slices of cake and to place them under their pillows that night — in the belief that they will dream of their future husbands; the best man warning them of the disastrous consequences that might overtake them if they happen to dream of some other man than their current boyfriends!

The Speeches

When the coffee stage is reached and the glasses needed for the toasts have been filled, the best man should call for order and introduce the first speaker. It is normally the bride's father whom he should call on to propose the toast of 'the health and happiness of the bride and bridegroom', but it is by no means uncommon for this duty to be passed to some other male member of the bride's family who is perhaps a better speaker or who happens to be someone of importance. However, it is only when the bride's father expressly asks someone else to speak on his behalf that someone may do so.

Care should be taken, too, to ensure that no-one is expected to deputise for the bride's father without due warning; even the best of speakers expect some time in which to gather together the material for their speeches.

The bridegroom replies on behalf of himself and his bride, taking the opportunity to thank his parents for their love and care during his boyhood, for the start they have given him in life − and for their good wishes for his future and that of his wife. The groom also takes this opportunity on behalf of his wife and himself to thank all those present for their gifts, and to invite them to come and see them in their new home.

Should there be any close members of the family who have not come to the wedding because of illness or other reasons, he should say how sorry he and his wife are that they are not present and to wish them a speedy recovery.

From this serious note, the bridegroom should now switch to a lighter note as he proposes the toast of the bridesmaids, and thanks them for a job well done. As a token of his appreciation, he may also present the bridesmaids with a small gift from himself and his wife.

It is the best man's duty to respond to this toast on

behalf of the bridesmaids. His speech should be light-hearted and joyful. It should be the 'high-spot' of the reception and it is very often his ability to make this particular speech, with humour and interest, that is the deciding consideration in his selection as best man. (See Chapter 13 for more information on the contents of his speech.)

These are the three accepted speeches usual to a wedding reception. No further speeches are required and as often as not, none is given.

Other speeches are, however, permissible; it is not unusual for the bridegroom's father to thank the host and hostess for the occasion and for the bride's father to reply — very briefly if he has already spoken.

Others may wish to speak, including ladies, but the best man must keep a wary eye on the clock.

A few suggestions for speeches are offered in Chapter 13, but they should only be used as a skeleton into which the speaker can introduce the personalities, the incidents and the jokes that will be understood by his audience.

Normally during the speeches the audience will, of course, be quiet and attentive. However, occasionally, there may be children present who are too young to understand the importance of remaining silent while others are speaking. In this event, the best man should politely request that the parents of the noisy children take them outside the reception room so that the rest of the audience can hear the speeches. Ideally, the parents should need no such request but should remove their children as soon as they start making a disturbance, but unfortunately we do not live in an ideal world and some parents are not always aware when their children are spoiling an occasion for others.

As soon as the best man judges that the speeches have run their course, or that it is time to bring them to an end, he should rise to his feet to read any telemessages of congratulations and good wishes which have been addressed to the bridal pair from their absent friends and relatives.

In reading these aloud to the assembled guests, the best man should do his best to add a few pithy comments concerning the contents and perhaps a few light references to the senders. If this is not done, this part of the proceedings can be very boring for the guests, especially if there are a lot of telemessages and a number of them have been sent by people unknown to the audience as a whole. In the event of receiving a large number of good luck messages, the best man can always list them together by saying 'N and M have also received best wishes from Aunti Vi in Australia, Robert, Sarah and Joanne in Texas, Emma and Michael in Aberdeen' and so on, keeping the original and humorous messages until the end. In order to keep the audience entertained, it has been known for best men to insert some pseudo messages such as:

From your bank manager: Keep up the interest rate.

From your stockbroker: Share and share alike for the best dividends.

From your doctor: Don't be an anti-body now.

From the groom's secretary: You're not the boss now.

After the reception — or more usually — after the honeymoon, the best man must see to it that these telemessages are passed to the bride. The safest place to lodge them is with the bride's mother − but it is the bride's duty to acknowledge them on her return from the honeymoon, usually at the same time as she writes to thank those who have sent her and her husband wedding gifts.

When the best man has finished reading the telemessages, the groom may wish to present the bride's mother and his own mother with a bouquet of flowers to thank them for all they have done to make the day so happy and memorable.

The reception proper is now over. It is time for the bride to retire with her chief bridesmaid to change from her wedding finery into her 'going away' clothes.

Traditionally, as she climbs the stairs to her changing room, her bridesmaids gather at the foot − or if there are no stairs, around the doorway through which she will pass to prepare for her departure. Everybody else should assemble behind the bridesmaids to watch as the bride throws her bouquet towards the bridesmaids. The young lady who captures the floral tribute is said, reputedly, to be the next bride. (Sometimes the bride throws her bouquet as she and her husband get into the car to leave for their honeymoon.)

At this stage, the best man should accompany the bridegroom to wherever he is to change for his honeymoon journey. If he has a changing room in the same building, the matter is a relatively simple affair, but if he has to rush home to change, there is no time to be wasted. He must be ready and waiting in the reception room when his wife returns, all ready to leave. If they are to leave by car for their destination, the luggage of the bride and groom will normally have been loaded in advance. If they are to depart by taxi, the

The bride throws her bouquet.

baggage should be assembled by the exit.

As soon as the bridegroom has changed, the best man should check and hand over to him all the necessary documents required for the honeymoon; rail, ferry or air tickets; passports, inoculation certificates, travellers' cheques, hotel reservations, timetables — and the marriage certificate if the bride has not already got it.

It is the job of the best man and the ushers to ensure that all the luggage is loaded aboard their transport, that

coats have not been forgotten, handbags overlooked —
and that they are still in time to catch their plane.

While the last of the farewells are being exchanged,
the honeymoon car will probably be being decorated
with balloons, a 'Just Married' sign, tin cans, foam and
various other paraphernalia.

Not until the newly-weds have finally departed should
the guests begin to leave. As they go, they should say
their farewells to their hosts (the parents of the bride),
followed by a parting word with the parents of the
bridegroom — until only they, the best man, the ushers,
bridesmaids and pages remain.

They have all gone.

12

And Afterwards

It is becoming more common for bride's and groom's homes to be far apart, so, very often, an evening entertainment is arranged. If relatives have come from afar, or the groom's parents are staying overnight in a nearby hotel, it is customary for the two sets of parents and any other relatives and friends to get together and either have an informal party at the bride's parents' home or go out to dinner, which will dispel any feeling of anti-climax after the newly-weds have left for their honeymoon.

Many bridal couples stay on and invite friends, who perhaps were not present at the main reception, to an evening disco.

The best man should not leave until all the celebrations are over and he can no longer find any task needing his attention. If the gifts have been on display, he may be asked to help pack them away and transport them to the newly-weds' home. He may also be expected to see the bridesmaids home.

It may be that the remains of the wedding cake need to be carefully packed and transported to the bride's parents' home, too. Her mother may wish to box and post portions of it to friends and relatives who were unable to attend the wedding — though it is quite in order for this task to be delayed until the bridal couple return from their honeymoon.

The bride's mother will undoubtedly gather together her daughter's wedding finery from the changing room, but the best man will need to perform the same service for the bridegroom.

Before finally leaving the reception rooms, the best

man should make a search to make sure that nothing has been left behind by the bridal couple, or the guests. Coats, umbrellas, gloves and so on should be taken to the home of the bride's mother. It is there that the forgetful guests will call when they miss their belongings.

The best man also has to remember to pack any hired suits he and the groom have been wearing and return them to the hirers.

13

Speeches

The best man can look forward to having to make two speeches in support of the bridegroom — the first at his stag party and the second at the reception after the wedding when he replies to the toast of the bridesmaids.

The second speech is, of course, much the more important of the two. It will have to be made to an audience consisting of the bride and bridegroom, the official attendants, the newly-weds' parents and the guests.

The first is the simpler of the two. It will be given to a limited number of listeners; all of them male, probably all of them of the same age group, and, no doubt, all of them friends of, and well-known to, the best man.

The main speech given at the stag party is usually made by the best man and is designed both to wish the bridegroom well in his forthcoming marriage and to deplore his departure from the ranks of his bachelor friends and, with tongue in cheek, to warn him of the perils he faces on the tidal waves of the deep sea of matrimony.

The best man should realise, when preparing his speech, that it must be light and amusing. The stag party is traditionally a high-spirited affair and by the time the best man is due to rise to his feet, the guests will probably have drunk a couple of rounds! For this reason, too, the guests at the party will be talkative and reluctant to spend too much time listening to someone else monopolising the conversation — however witty he may be. In other words, he must be brief.

A speech that might be typical of what is expected could start:

'It is a sad, sad occasion when a man decides to desert the friends of his youth and surrender himself to the machinations of a female. Yet here tonight we are witness to one who has the cheek to bribe us with a meal and a bottle of wine, not to forget him after he has gone, and to offer up unending prayers for his salvation.

'My friends, look at him sitting there at the head of the table, bleary eyed and without a thought for the group of wailing women I passed on the doorstep as I came in tonight — abandoned, betrayed and broken-hearted. Is his bride aware of these luckless girls? Or are these cigars the price of our silence? But let us not despise the weakling too deeply. Let us remember, what he appears to have overlooked, that the down-payment on a bride is as nothing to the upkeep thereafter. She will require three pairs of shoes to his one, a dozen pairs of tights to his couple of pairs of socks, and a choice of fifty dresses and skirts whilst he travels to town in the same old suit.

'And is that the full tale of financial ruin? Not on your life; just as he decides that he must seek additional employment in the evenings to keep pace with his debts, she will present him with a wailing demander of milk, nappies and transport.

'However, I have good news for him. His friends will remember him with sympathy as they imbibe their accustomed pints at the local on a Saturday night. Indeed, we shall drink an extra at the very thought of him having to stay at home to wash the dishes, repair the drains and paper the walls. We shall weep into this extra glass of beer — at the thought that he is not there to pay for it.

'Of course, he knows full well that despite these sombre warnings, we do wish him well for the future — but if he should want to escape it, let him know that we are prepared to have a whip round for cash with which to feed his gas meter; or if he should think enough of his friends to want to spare them the dreary trail behind a hearse, they will gladly cut a hole in the ice on the duck pond, large enough for him to slip through.

'If even these escape routes fail to appeal to him, let us, as a last resort, wish him all the joys of a softer shoulder on which to cry, warmed slippers of an evening by his chair, no more buttonless shirts, a full half share in his own car — and no more need for chilly goodbyes on the girlfriend's doorstep. Lift your glasses everybody and let's sing "For he's a jolly good fellow".'

The only other obligatory speech of the evening should be the reply from the bridegroom — equally light, amusing and — brief.

There are three customary speeches at the reception

following the wedding, though only the time available need restrict others from speaking. These are:

1. From the bride's father who proposes the toast of 'The happiness and prosperity of the bride and bridegroom'.

2. The reply from the bridegroom, following which he proposes 'The health and happiness of the bridesmaids'.

3. The best man replies on behalf of the bridesmaids.

Only the third of these speeches directly concerns the best man, but as he may be asked by others for a few things concerning their own speeches, it will not be out of place here to list some of the thoughts that should be expressed by them.

Where the bride's father proposes the toast to the bridal couple, he should make reference to:

(a) The joy he and his wife have had in the bringing up of their daughter (including a couple of happy incidents of her childhood), and how sadly they will miss her from their home.

(b) The pleasure they have found in getting to know their new son-in-law − and his parents.

(c) The certainty they feel that in her husband's care, their daughter will prosper along with him − and with a little homily on the 'give and take' necessary to a successful marriage − the confidence they have that happiness must accompany the love they so evidently bear for one another.

The bridegroom's reply on behalf of his wife and himself should include:

(a) His gratitude for the care and love he has had at the hands of his parents since he could remember (including one or two memories of the happy days he has experienced in his boyhood and youth).

(b) His gratitude for the start they have given him for his new life. His education, his training towards a livelihood — and where applicable, for the gifts he and his wife have received from them and everyone else towards setting up their new home.

(c) He should express his gratitude, on behalf of his wife and himself, for her father's good wishes — perhaps bringing out the old adage of 'not having lost a daughter, but gained a son'.

At this point the bridegroom should switch to a brighter theme with the toast of 'the bridesmaids'.

(d) He may congratulate them on getting his bride to the wedding on time.

(e) He might remark on their good looks and happy demeanour — and their prospects of being inundated with 'male admirers' and the inevitable result.

He may interrupt his speech to give each of the bridesmaids in turn a small gift, going from one to the other to do so, though often if they are presented with lockets, these are given beforehand and worn for the wedding. Then returning to his bride, he should conclude with:

(f) The toast, 'The bridesmaids'.

It is the best man's duty to reply on behalf of the bridesmaids. His speech should be free of all solemnity and designed to add to the note of light entertainment introduced by the bridegroom.

The only way of achieving an apparently effortless and amusing speech is by putting a great deal of effort into its preparation. If he puts off thinking about it until the evening before the wedding, it will probably be a dismal failure! If the result is to be a success, it needs proper planning.

As soon as he is asked to be best man, he should start jotting down amusing and apt stories about weddings, any incidents he remembers or has been told about the bridegroom in his youth, or more recently. Note down some of the triumphs in the bridegroom's life — sporting, academic or career. How did the couple meet? Is there a story there? Is the bride a very organised person, the opposite of the groom? Is the groom a better cook than his wife-to-be? All these things are possible sources of ideas for the speech. When he has several pages of notes, he can start to write his speech. It should have a beginning, a middle and an end.

The beginning should be amusing, and arresting enough to capture his audience's attention and will probably deal with the bride and groom's triumphs, achievements and antics.

The middle will include the goodwill and best wishes from their friends and relatives, how suited they are and the changes likely to take place in the habits of the groom — such as washing up every day instead of once a month.

The best man can write down the main headings on a postcard.

The best man can also warn the bride, in a joking way, of any particular idiosyncrasies that her husband has, such as being allergic to morning, or work, or alarm clocks.

The end of the speech should be a message of hope for the future, perhaps presented as a quotation if a suitable one can be found.

Having written it out, he will probably find it is far too long and will then have to start pruning it.

It is always a good idea to read it aloud — he can

then hear which bits can be cut out, and if he does it in front of a mirror it should remind him not to look too serious or to pull faces. If he finds it difficult to memorise the whole speech, rather than reading it out (which will sound rather stilted), he can use a postcard and write down the main headings, with words that will jog his memory about a particular story or idea to be included. Make sure that all notes are in large print so that each item can be picked out without having to search through them.

If he is still not sure about his speech, he should try it out on a friend, and be sure to speak slowly and clearly. It is always better to be brief than to ramble on endlessly.

He might write:

'I have known, to my cost (the bridegroom) for a very long time and though I have not had the pleasure of knowing (the bride) for so long, I am sure that their happiness is certain. My only regret is that it wasn't I who met (the bride) first — or at any rate in sufficient time to warn her of (the bridegroom's) idiosyncrasies — to divert her attentions — elsewhere.

'Here, yet again, is an example of the luck some men get — whether they deserve it or not and of what some girls fall for! Whilst others of us ...

'I can assure (the bride) of (the bridegroom's) devotion; I have had the most trying time today getting him ready for his wedding. Not because of any reluctance on his part, but because of the times I have had to answer such questions as 'Do you think she'll change her mind at the last minute?' or 'Are we going to be late?' or 'Have you forgotten the ring?'

'As if my thoughts weren't already heavily engaged with my duties to the bridesmaids! If, for instance, the best man is allowed to kiss the bride, is he also allowed to kiss the bridesmaids? A wishful thought perhaps — but one that is inclined to distract attention from the less attractive job of seeing that the bridegroom has braced his trousers up to the correct height and cleaned his shoes first.

'If you will glance at the bridesmaids you will understand why I accepted the duties of a best man. Who could possibly deny themselves the opportunity of being associated with them — and who will forget in a very long time their beauty and vivaciousness? I thank you all for your good wishes on their behalf and hope you enjoy the rest of this happy day.'

He might write himself notes on this speech as follows:

HOW LONG I'VE KNOWN ...

PITY I DIDN'T MEET HIS WIFE FIRST.

BRIDEGROOM'S DEVOTION — WILL SHE COME?

WHAT IMPEDIMENT COULD THERE BE?

RING — FIFTY TIMES.

CAN I KISS BRIDESMAIDS AND BRIDE? RATHER THAN CLEAN (THE BRIDEGROOM'S) SHOES.

THANKS FOR GOOD WISHES TO BRIDESMAIDS.

Other speeches may follow, but none is obligatory. If time permits, toasts may be offered to:

(a) The health of the bridegroom's parents.

(b) The health of the bride's parents.

The build-up of each speech should reflect the mood of the reception and the character of him who makes it, but it should be remembered that a wedding is very much a family occasion and wider issues should not be introduced – even where the marriage is a public affair.

Be brief. Many of the family and guests may not have met for a very long time and will want to talk about their lives between. Many still will want a chance of a word with the newly-weds before they have to rush off on their honeymoon journey. And the bride herself needs time to change into her 'going away' outfit.

A valuable source of material for speeches is the companion book in the *Right Way* series "Wedding Speeches – a Book of Example Speeches" by Gordon Stretch (uniform with this book). This contains 65 example speeches of which 15 are specifically for the best man.

14

Anniversaries

Anniversaries of a wedding are almost always a matter of remembrance between the man and his wife — and too often forgotten by everyone else. Even the couple themselves soon find themselves treating the annual event casually. Perhaps an exchange of gifts, maybe a night out — and very often a mere 'happy anniversary' wish is the only 'celebration'.

Of course, as the years go by, the responsibilities of a growing family tend to detract from the interest of 'fading' memories. Schooling, mumps, children's birthdays, holidays, and in due course children's engagements and weddings! Grandchildren more mumps, more birthdays ...

However, it is the custom — though rarely followed today — for the best man to remind the couple of their anniversaries with an 'anniversary' card, or perhaps a floral tribute. Nothing more is required as any celebrations are regarded as being the private affair of the couple — and the best man may only expect, if his memento is more than a card, no more than a cheerful acknowledgement.

After a very few years, even this small reminder by the best man is inclined to lapse. Probably he too has married and is becoming deeply embroiled in the ties of a growing family of his own. School holidays, children's Christmas parties, chicken pox ...

But as long as he remains single, a best man should not altogether forget his friend's anniversary. Even if it becomes no more than a telephone call, the 'bride' at least will appreciate the thought.

And still the years gather dust — until the best man is faced with an invitation to his friend's Silver Wedding party! Probably only then does he realise that twenty-five years have gone by since he stood at his friend's side, facing the altar.

It is the 'bridal couple's' duty to send out the invitations for this anniversary party. A service in the church where they were married may start the day, but the main celebrations will probably take place in the evening.

A dinner party, perhaps followed by a visit to a theatre or a night-club or a dance, may be the order of the day. But whatever it is, the scale and scope of the party will rest with the couple, whose financial situation and the size of their family may dictate the venue and the type of entertainment they offer.

The invitations will normally include:

Sons and daughters.

Wives and husbands of the above.

Best man and his wife.

Chief bridesmaid and her husband.

The 'bride's' parents.

The 'bridegroom's' parents.

Guests at the wedding who are or have become very close friends; the numbers depending on the total number that can be accommodated at the party.

After twenty-five years there are likely to be many gaps in the above list. Parents may have passed on, others may now live far away — and some, whose present addresses have been forgotten, will be lost in the mists of time.

Formal wear is only preferred where the couple are in a substantial position in life, in which event it should be copied by all the guests — and guests must be prepared for this, by asking when the invitations are accepted. Of course, if the invitations are in writing, the form of dress should be mentioned on the card.

Informality is more usual today, even though the party may be held in a restaurant or hotel.

A wedding cake — small — should be on the table, but as it is not the custom to send portions to absent friends, none of it need be saved. In due course, it should be cut in the same token fashion as on the occasion of the original wedding reception, twenty-five years ago.

Speeches are usually few and happy. The first is normally made by the couple's eldest son in the form of a toast to their 'continued happiness'. The husband is expected to reply on behalf of his wife and himself.

Where there is no son, the best man normally proposes the toast.

If there does happen to be a son, the best man is

expected to make a speech following that of the husband. This should be full of cheerful reminiscenes, probably new to the sons and daughters of the couple − and perhaps a few amusing comparisons between the way of life today and as it was lived a quarter of a century ago.

Silver wedding gifts are given as convenient; some before the party and others as the guests arrive. They should all be of silver, or where that is not feasible, because of cost, particularly in the case of presents from young children, they should be tied up with silver ribbon.

In any event, silver is acceptable in the form of silver plate, and should not therefore be an embarrassment to impecunious guests.

More years pass by and, before you know it, fifty years have elapsed since the wedding, and the couple are celebrating their Golden Wedding.

It is customary for the eldest son − or daughter − to organise a small party to celebrate their parents' Golden Wedding. The guests will comprise the couple's family; sons, daughters, their wives and husbands, grandchildren, probably with their wives and husbands − and as guests of honour, if they are still available, the best man and chief bridesmaid who were in attendance at that wedding so long ago.

The announcement of the Golden Wedding will probably be made in the press and no doubt the best man will receive his invitation to the party either by letter or telephone.

The party may be held, without formality, at the couple's home, in one of their children's homes or some hotel or restaurant. There should be a wedding cake of only sufficient size for the purpose, and in due time the

The Golden Wedding.

bridal couple will cut it as they did the original cake fifty years ago.

This time the presents should be of 'gold', though very often they are much less valuable and merely consist of token gifts tied with 'gold' ribbon. This is particularly apt where the presents are from young great-grandchildren. As the couple either possess (or no longer require) gifts of intrinsic value, flowers tied with a ribbon of 'gold' are an ideal tribute from the best man and the chief bridesmaid.

Speeches are not essential — except for perhaps a toast to the 'happy couple' and a brief reply from the bridegroom.

The last, or almost certainly the last, duty of a best man is to attend the Diamond Wedding of the same couple — if they and he have survived the sixty years that have fled by since the first wedding. The party will be small and similar to that held in celebration of their Golden Wedding.

Presents rarely include diamonds as it can be assumed that valuable gifts are no longer of very great importance to their recipients; flowers are by far the most suitable gifts.

The party will be organised by the couple's family who should make sure that any elderly guests are escorted home afterwards.

It must be rare indeed for the ultimate wedding celebration to be attended by the best man and the chief bridesmaid. In fact, as this second 'Diamond Wedding' is the seventy-fifth anniversary of the wedding, it must be equally rare for all the parties to survive and be available to attend the party.

Nevertheless, the author of this book wishes, with all sincerity, that the best man who scans these pages will celebrate the climax of his duties at such an occasion.

As a matter of interest, anniversaries of a wedding are traditionally known as:

1st anniversary	Paper
2nd anniversary	Cotton
3rd anniversary	Leather
4th anniversary	Silk
5th anniversary	Wood
6th anniversary	Iron
7th anniversary	Wool
8th anniversary	Bronze
9th anniversary	Pottery
10th anniversary	Tin
12th anniversary	Linen
15th anniversary	Crystal
20th anniversary	China
25th anniversary	SILVER
30th anniversary	Pearl or Ivory
35th anniversary	Coral
40th anniversary	Ruby
45th anniversary	Sapphire
50th anniversary	GOLD
55th anniversary	Emerald
60th anniversary	DIAMOND
75th anniversary	and again, DIAMOND

15

When The Best Man's A Woman

It is unusual, but perfectly possible, for the bridegroom to choose a woman as his best 'man'. He must be aware, however, that he is asking her to play an unusual role, and he must make sure that everyone involved in the ceremony is comfortable with the situation.

It is the bride's special day, and she must have the final say. If she doesn't want to see another woman sitting next to her future husband as she walks down the aisle, she must feel free to say so. But if both bride and groom are happy with the choice of a sister or female friend as 'best woman', then the idea can add a little novelty to the traditional ceremonies. (Don't under *any* circumstances, let the groom's ex-girlfriend be best woman. It is unfair to everyone.)

The bride and groom need to consider the same points as they would for any other best man:

Is she well organised?

Can she make a clear, brief and amusing speech?

Is she happy to take on this responsibility?

Assuming she agrees, there are still several issues to decide.

Dress
Traditionally the best man dresses in almost identical clothes to those of the groom. The best woman is unlikely to want to do so; however, she must be readily identifiable in her role. A formal suit, with a buttonhole matching those of the ushers or the groom, should distinguish her from the other guests. Black or grey are not necessary; navy is possible, or greyish purple, or olive.

The Stag Night
A best woman really can't act as an honorary man on this occasion. The groom should either organise his own stag party (men only), or have a mixed singles party, if he wants the best woman to be present.

Who Does What?
The best woman will probably wish to pass on to an usher (or other suitable man) the duties of carrying suitcases, calming the groom down the night before his wedding, and helping him get dressed. She could share accommodation with the bridesmaids overnight and join the groom about an hour before the wedding.

Remember to let the photographer, and the vicar or minister, know who is who!

The Speech
The best woman has to be even more tactful than a best

man. If she is a friend of the groom, not a relative, she must avoid giving the impression that she ever wanted to take the bride's place. She may refer – briefly – to her unusual role, perhaps using it as an introduction to an anecdote about the groom's idiosyncrasies. Otherwise, the usual guidelines for a best man still apply.

INDEX